Dreamtime Heritage

AUSTRALIAN ABORIGINAL MYTHS

DREAMTIME HERITAGE

AUSTRALIAN ABORIGINAL MYTHS
IN PAINTINGS BY **AINSLIE ROBERTS**
AND TEXT BY **MELVA JEAN ROBERTS**

Line Illustrations by Ainslie Roberts

THE DREAMTIME SERIES
The Dreamtime (first published 1965, reprinted nineteen times)
The Dawn of Time (1969, reprinted sixteen times)
The First Sunrise (1971, reprinted twelve times)
The Dreamtime Book (1973, reprinted eleven times)
Dreamtime Heritage (1975, reprinted seven times)
Dreamtime, The Aboriginal Heritage (1981, reprinted four times)
Dreamtime Stories for Children (1983, reprinted four times)
Ainslie Roberts and the Dreamtime (1988)
Echoes of the Dreamtime (1988)

Published by Art Australia, 4 Edgecumbe Parade, Blackwood 5051,
South Australia, Australia, 1989.
National Library of Australia
Cataloguing-in-Publication entry
Roberts, Ainslie, 1911-
    Dreamtime heritage: Australian Aboriginal myths in paintings.
    ISBN 1 875168 03 6.
    1. Roberts, Ainslie, 1911-   . 2. Painting, Australian.
    [3]. Aborigines, Australian – Legends. 4. Art and mythology.
    I. Roberts, Melva Jean. II. Title. III. Title: Dreamtime, the
    Aboriginal heritage: Australian Aboriginal myths in paintings.
759.994
Designed by Ainslie Roberts.
Printed by Griffin Press Ltd., Adelaide.
Distributed by Gary Allen Pty. Ltd., Sydney.

TO THE ABORIGINAL PEOPLE
who handed down these Dreamtime Myths

CONTENTS

DREAMTIME HERITAGE

THE MYSTICAL CONDITIONS KNOWN TO ABORIGINES collectively as the Dreamtime, and to an individual as his Dreaming, defy rational explanation to people reared in a Western-style civilisation. Nevertheless it is possible for such people to understand with their hearts even if they reject the evidence presented by their minds.

Primitive instincts lie buried in even the most sophisticated adult, and in those blurred areas of the mind known as the unconscious there are powerful forces which most of us glimpse from time to time. The difference between ourselves and tribal Aborigines is that we have erected barriers of logic which prevent us from seeing clearly into our own Dreaming.

The Dreaming of each Aboriginal encompassed everything with which he had been associated since the dawn of consciousness. Before that, it extended into the Dreamtime. His Dreaming was a blend of many different factors and influences partaking of both spiritual and physical life, bound together so tightly that it became the core of his being.

His Dreaming included the laws of nature, of his totem, and of his tribe. It comprised his weapons and his skill in using them, his cunning as a hunter and courage as a warrior, and his obligations to people of every age group within his tribe. In the emotional sense it was confirmed by his initiation into the age-old rites and ceremonies. It guided his hand as he worked with wood or stone, inspired him artistically in painting, carving, and body decoration, and leapt within his body as he performed the songs and dances to placate or worship the unseen powers.

Interwoven with all these factors was the feeling which every creature knows in greater or lesser degree: that which has been called the Spirit of Place. Biologists believe that birds are "imprinted" with this feeling within an hour of being hatched, so that for the rest of their lives they are able to return unerringly to their birthplace. Other animals, and all people living in a state of nature, feel it with an instinctive strength. We who have surrendered our instincts to technology feel it only vaguely, though most people feel themselves to be more "at home" in one specific place than any other in the world. This feeling pervaded the consciousness of tribal Aborigines to such depths that it dictated their entire way of life.

A man's Dreaming merged with the Dreamtime. Everything in life, whether tangible or intangible, had been influenced by the people of the Dreamtime: the creators of the world and those who lived in the beginning. Therefore, everything that he saw, did, felt, and experienced was to some degree sacred. The landscape in which an Aboriginal lived was shaped in the form he could observe because the Dreamtime people made it so. Countless features had a Dreamtime explanation: the exploits of Dreamtime heroes and villains had influenced the shape of rocks, the colours of the earth, the windings of a watercourse. Such features were tangible memorials of his tribe's creative ancestors and mainstays of its emotional life.

Together with these unchanging features there were those which showed a periodic change. The seasons of the year; the heavenly bodies; the light and shade which varied with each moment of the day; the ages of man; birth, life, and death. All of these had specific reasons for the ways in which they manifested themselves, and the reasons were enshrined in the stories of the Dreamtime.

The same applied to every living creature, whether bird, fish, mammal, insect, plant, or reptile. Many of them, in the Dreamtime, had been Aborigines or had acted under the impulse of human emotions. Their deeds or misdeeds during the creation era are reflected by their behaviour in non-human form. Each of them must forever conform to a pattern established in the Dreamtime, and these patterns could always be found in the body of Dreamtime lore handed down by the storytellers.

The emotional impact of this body of lore was immense. Its overall effect was one of complete security. A man knew, always and forever, his exact place in society and in his physical and spiritual world.

As he grew from infancy into adolescence and passed through maturity into old age he knew that he would advance through the hierarchy of his tribe, with rights which no one questioned and obligations to be automatically fulfilled. He belonged to a totem which dictated the woman he could marry, the creatures he could hunt, and the ceremonies he should perform. He lived in a tribal area reserved to him and his people, with the secure knowledge that no one would ever challenge his right to be there. He would not leave it, or permit others to enter, without negotiations performed in accordance with ancient laws. And he knew that if he transgressed any of the laws of his community, punishment was inevitable.

In all these circumstances, he moved through life with the supreme confidence of a man who knows that he is surrounded by the spiritual beings who established his world. He was not called upon to believe in an unseen god: he could see proof positive of the beings in which he believed. He saw their marks on the earth. He observed them, in the form of plants and animals, obeying the patterns laid down for them in the Dreamtime. He felt them in the changes of the seasons and watched them as they moved through the skies in the form of sun, moon, stars, planets, and clouds. All life was one and he was a part of life, bound immutably within the great design worked out for him by his creation ancestors.

This design was unchanged for thousands of years, until it was shattered, in the twinkling of an eye, by the invaders who forced the tribesmen to accept a new way of life.

During the "fatal impact" of Europeans on many other races, from Incas to Tahitians, a myriad age-old cultures were shattered or perverted. The tragedy of the Aborigines is that, during the period in which they broke under the impact, only a few Europeans had sufficient insight to discern the subtle depths of Aboriginal culture. The Aborigines were regarded as a kind of animal: the only dangerous animal on the continent, and predators upon the settlers' flocks and herds. They did not even have the romantic aura of Red Indians or South Sea islanders or the martial glamour of the Zulus and Maoris. Their art was weird and primitive to the sophisticated eye. Their crafts were limited to the simple use of natural materials. If they had any social organisation it was not easily apparent. They were Stone Age man.

As such, they were swept aside. They had nothing tangible to offer, they made poor servants, and they were of no use to Europeans intent upon making their fortunes. The tragedy is that when so many of the Aboriginal tribes were eliminated, they took with them one of mankind's last opportunities to study the very wellsprings of the human race.

It is now known that a thriving Aboriginal culture existed in Australia as much as 35,000 years ago, and possibly even earlier. This is not guesswork, but a fact proven by the carbon-dating process which enables scientists to fix an exact age upon bones and artefacts. But these remains cannot speak. They can act only as parts of a jigsaw puzzle, to be laboriously pieced together by anthropologists. But less than two centuries ago it would have been possible to talk directly to the inheritors of a culture reaching back through the mists of time, preserved almost intact within a continent which showed, by countless examples of its flora and fauna, that it was utterly different from the rest of the world.

That opportunity was lost. Nowadays, when white Australians have awoken to a dramatic awareness of the people who lived here before us, we must attempt to peer through the mists by interpreting the few remaining clues. Among the most colourful and revealing are the stories of the Dreamtime.

The most intriguing aspect of these stories is that so many of them, including some collected in this volume and others in its series, show a close relationship to the spiritual inheritance of other peoples of the world. The most obvious example is the recurrence of a Creator, or of what must be loosely termed the Creation Ancestors, in one after another of the Dreamtime tales. This being takes a variety of forms, and acts in a variety of ways. But there is always a basic resemblance between the Creator in the Dreamtime stories and the creator who is a dominant figure in the religions or folklores of other lands. In the Bible it is Jehovah, the creator who spoke to Moses out of a burning bush. In one of the stories in this book, the Ancestor spoke to the Aborigines from the trunk of a great tree, and for much the same reason that Jehovah sometimes spoke to his people. They had strayed from the path of righteousness, and were afraid and lonely because they had ignored the immutable laws.

Most of the great religions of the world, and some of the lesser ones, follow much the same theme. In the beginning there was nothing until a mysterious creator formed heaven and earth, ocean, land, and all their creatures. The Aborigines had this belief and the story "In the Beginning" gives explicit details of the Creator's activities. When he decided to create man he used clay, the very material used as a synonym for the transient nature of man in some Christian doctrine.

It may be argued that it is somewhat sacrilegious to compare the enshrined lore of the great religions of Europe and Asia with those of the primitive nomads of Australia. The idea that anyone could truly believe in the Rainbow Serpent, the great snake who ascended into the skies, may seem ridiculous. Yet hundreds of millions of Christians found no difficulty in believing implicitly that a snake spoke to Eve, that the sun stood still for Joshua and the Red Sea parted for Moses, that angels spoke from the sky and a child was born to a virgin. These and similar miracles are pillars of the Christian faith, and, even though modern thought may offer rational explanations, a belief in such miracles brought comfort to countless people over the centuries.

Perhaps the most important thing is that mankind should believe in something: that out of the struggling mystery of his life he should use the mysterious powers of imagination to create some guideposts whereby his spiritual life can find direction. This is exactly what the Aborigines did in their Dreamtime stories. The fascinating thing is that, in so many ways, they shimmer upon the edges of beliefs similar to those held by other religions. When the whole of mankind lived in the Stone Age, then perhaps these Dreamtime stories were the common currency of belief. If so, then the other races of the world followed them along different paths while the Aborigines, locked away from the world in their forgotten continent, preserved these beliefs intact.

A number of the stories, like those of the Old Testament, are moral parables which deal with the lusts of the flesh and the darker emotions of mankind. The Biblical story of Cain and Abel stresses the fact that brothers do not necessarily love one another: that of "The Fighting Brothers" does the same. The basic principle of all religions is that life does not cease after death, but it is rarely described as beautifully as in the Aboriginal myth "Birth of the Butterflies," which tells how re-incarnation was deduced from the metamorphosis of caterpillars into butterflies. Primitive men in every land would have seen the same example of life returning, in a different form, to creatures apparently dead. Perhaps the story of the butterflies inspired some long-forgotten race to a belief in the theory of life after death, and thus to the foundation of a religion from which all others have stemmed. There is certainly a close link between religion and natural phenomena. The festival of Easter uses an egg as the symbol of rebirth.

Apart from these religious parallels, which cannot be proved or disproved, Aboriginal mythology has a relationship to the mythology of most other lands. Both employ similar plots and characters. A common tale is that of the mysterious monster which kills any human who ventures into its domain. In this book it is exemplified by the tale "Naruwilya and the Intruder." Another myth construction, common to many races, is based upon unconsummated love. Some tragic inter-vention prevents young lovers from coming together, and so their love is magically perpetuated by a natural feature. The story of "Condula and Bak-bak" is typical of this style.

Greek and Roman mythology have many heroes possessed of magical or superhuman powers, which they used sometimes for community benefit and sometimes for personal gain. The Aboriginal stories "Karkan and the Valley of Blood," "Koolulla and the Two Sisters," and "The Transformation of Burnba," are reminiscent of these. They have the same theme of human lust and envy, and perhaps the original story-tellers were inspired by similar emotions. Most people have dreamed of achieving their ends by some mysterious bounty of strength, cunning, or good fortune.

Another series of myths encountered in other countries is that which explains natural phenomena by mystical causes. Aboriginal mythology has a similar body of beliefs. In this book the stories of the thunder-men Jambuwul and Mamaragan, and "The First Dawn" and "The Creation of Black Mountain," typify myths which give mystical explanations for natural phenomena.

The belief that people of all nations share the same mythical life is not new and has been explored exhaustively. And, despite the cold logic of science, mythical and mystical beliefs have an abiding appeal and spiritual comfort for much of mankind.

The fascination of Aboriginal mythology is that these "Stone Age" men preserved a complex spiritual culture in which the Dreamtime myths, an integral part of this culture, may without any great stretch of the imagination be associated with the mystical life of peoples in other parts of the world. From this, one may play with the corollary that Aboriginal mythology derives not only from the Dreamtime of the Aborigines, but from the Dreamtime of the human race as a whole. It is not difficult to believe that the Aborigines, isolated on a continent which some scientists believe was once connected to the rest of the world, maintained a spiritual culture at one time common to all humanity but since diverted into many different channels.

If this is so, then the Dreamtime stories may demonstrate a deeper brotherhood than we are yet willing to concede. It is a brotherhood stretching back to the very dawn of time, when all men were of one race and all sought the keys to mysteries which still remain concealed.

THE FIGHTING BROTHERS

Long ago, on Victoria's western coast, there lived two brothers who had hunted and fished together since childhood. Pupadi, the elder, was the one who always speared the most game, knew the best fishing spots, and was looked upon as the camp favourite. Gerdang, the younger, secretly resented his secondary role. His jealousy increased when Pupadi took a wife, because she was the woman whom Gerdang most desired.

Gerdang's longing for his brother's wife became so fierce that he begged her to run away with him. When she refused, Gerdang took her by force and carried her far to the east, where a great shelf of rock runs into the sea.

Pupadi returned from hunting, and knew what had taken place because he was aware of Gerdang's envy. In a violent rage he followed their tracks and found them. He attacked Gerdang, and they fought for many hours until the younger brother ran into the scrub and hid. Pupadi climbed a large rock to gain a better view, but Gerdang circled behind him and threw a boomerang with such force that it buried itself deep between his brother's shoulder-blades and knocked him into the bushes at the cliff's edge.

Reckless with triumph, and expecting to find his brother dead, Gerdang leapt into the bushes. But Pupadi, calling on the last of his strength, lay on his stomach with his spear held upwards. Gerdang jumped straight on to it, to die with the barbed point sticking out of his back.

The impact carried them over the cliff, and Pupadi fell into the sea and became the shark. The big fin on his back is his brother's boomerang, still deeply embedded. Gerdang hit a shelf of rock with such force that his body was flattened, and in this form the tide carried it away as the stingray, with Pupadi's spear changed into the barbed sting at the base of the tail. The blow-holes along the cliff top were made by the stamping feet of the fighting brothers.

KARKAN AND THE VALLEY OF BLOOD

Karkan was a man of fine build and a great hunter. His tribe admired these qualities but they disliked his vanity and conceit. When Winju, a modest and likeable man, came to stay with the tribe, the friendliness extended to him made Karkan so frenzied with jealousy that he made plans to kill him. So Karkan persuaded Winju to go hunting, and on the night before they set out he sharpened a number of hardwood sticks at both ends. He took these to a place where there were many kangaroo-rats, and pushed them into the earth, points upwards, in the tall grass. Karkan also tied a cord around some of the grass and trailed it to a near-by bush, and then his trap was ready for Winju.

When the two hunters reached the spot, Karkan told Winju that his method of catching the kangaroo-rat was to run to the spot where movement showed in the grass, then jump so that he could land on the animal with both feet. As he said this he twitched the cord so that the grass quivered. The trusting Winju jumped into the grass and drove the sticks deep into his feet and legs. For many days Winju, in his agony, thrashed and crawled about until he had made a deep valley, and his blood stained the whole area red.

But because Winju was a good man, his ancestral spirits restored him to health and great strength. Some days later, Karkan had only a brief glimpse of his rival before Winju's spear killed him. The body fell into the camp-fire and sparks flew in all directions. They started a bushfire which swept over most of the country, and from the ashes a brown bird rose to hover above the same spot day after day.

The Aborigines of the Coolgardie area believed that the blood shed by Winju created the precious red ochre, used for body decoration, in the sacred source which they knew as the Valley of Blood. The brown bird is a kestrel, destined to keep watch on the ground forever because it contains the spirit of Karkan, still wary of another surprise attack by Winju.

Karkan and the Valley of Blood.

Mr Cameron R. Sands

THE ORIGIN OF THE PLATYPUS

Naruni, youngest and most beautiful woman in her tribe, had been promised in marriage to a tribal elder. But she was attracted to the younger and more attractive Kuralka, who persuaded her to run away with him to the hills country. After many months the pair became conscience-stricken and returned to the tribe in disgrace. Naruni was transformed into a duck, and Kuralka was punished by being changed into a giant water-rat. Both were banished to a far-distant river.

Rejected by the land and her people, Naruni in due course hatched two eggs. To her horror, she found that they did not contain ducklings, but strange creatures with bodies of fur, webbed feet, and duck bills.

So great was Naruni's disappointment, and so strong was her yearning for the solid ground and her lost tribal life, that she pined away and died. But her two children thrived in their watery home, and multiplied to establish the platypus family.

This is how the Aborigines explained the origin of the platypus to the early settlers of New South Wales, and they also described its habits and how it reproduced. When the first platypus skin was shown to European scientists it caused a sensation, and they were so astonished that they said the beak and feet of water birds had been sewn to the skin of some animal.

After that, controversy raged for eighty years over how the platypus produced its young, until it was proved that the creature laid eggs and suckled its offspring. This strange link in the biological chain is unique to Australia.

The myth in which Aborigines explained the origin of the platypus is characteristic of the way in which they used fantasy to account for phenomena which baffled scientists.

The Origin of the Platypus

LINGA OF AYERS ROCK

This myth, handed down by the Pitjandjara tribe, relates how Linga, a little lizard-man, lived by himself near the place where Ayers Rock (Uluru) now stands. Linga had spent many days making a boomerang, and when it was finished he threw it to test its balance. The boomerang flew higher and higher into the air and spun across the desert until it buried itself in the soft sand of the great red sandhill from which Ayers Rock was later created.

Greatly distressed at the loss of such a fine weapon, Linga hurried to the spot and dug everywhere with his bare hands to find it. Today, many of the spectacular features of Ayers Rock are the result of Linga's frantic digging. The deep holes and gutters, which he made in the sand, have since been transformed into large pot-holes and vertical chasms in the steep face of the huge monolith.

Linga, forever associated with the sand in which he lost his boomerang, became the little sand-lizard. And, if you are quiet enough, and quick enough, you may surprise him alongside a small hole in some red sandhill.

If, in awe, you wonder how he survives in such an arid region, your curiosity is a tribute to the Aborigines of the desert. For countless thousands of years, and with only five simple tools, they gained an adequate living in an environment so harsh that no white man could live there unless he carried his own food and water.

Linga of Ayers Rock

Ainslie Roberts
1972

THE CREATION OF THE JENOLAN CAVES

The Aborigines of New South Wales believed that, in the Dreamtime, Mirragan the hunter tried to spear Gurangatch, a huge half-fish, half-reptile which lived in a deep waterhole in the Wollondilly River. After failing many times, Mirragan tried to poison the water with hickory bark. But Gurangatch escaped by tearing up the ground along a near-by valley, so that the water in the river flowed along after him.

Mirragan was relentless in his ambition to capture such a large creature, and he caught up with Gurangatch many times. Each time they fought fiercely, but each time Gurangatch escaped. Finally he burrowed into the mountains and created a huge cave.

The determined Mirragan then climbed to the top of the range, and drove his spear deep into the ground to frighten Gurangatch out of the cave. He drove his spear down in many places, and each time Gurangatch dug further into the mountains until he had created a labyrinth of caves. At last he broke out on the other side and disappeared into the Joolundoo waterhole. Mirragan returned with the tribe's best divers, but none of them could dislodge the creature from this deepest of all waterholes.

The encounter between Mirragan and Gurangatch resulted in the formation of the Wollondilly and the Cox rivers, the Jenolan and Whambeyan caves, the blowholes on top of the Blue Mountains and, in the places where they fought, the many deep waterholes in the two rivers.

The Aborigines always avoided these waterholes, believing that they were inhabited by the descendants of Gurangatch.

Creation of the Jonahan Caves —   Airli Roberts

THE CAPTURE OF FIRE

Many different types of terrain and climate may be found within the continent of Australia, and because Aboriginal beliefs were intimately associated with the type of country in which the tribes lived, many myths with a common basis varied according to the locality.

One of the most important factors in Aboriginal life was fire and its benefits. There are many different stories explaining how it was first obtained. Some stories say that a bird brought it to the people, others describe a tribesman's dangerous journey to obtain fire from a burning mountain, and in some myths the gift of fire resulted from lightning which set fire to a tree.

Most fire-myth variations share common themes of greed and reprisal. There is a selfish person who discovers the secret of fire, but keeps it to himself, and there are those who use courage and ingenuity to take it from him so that it can be shared.

A fire-myth from the Murrumbidgee region is typical of this construction. It says that Goodah, a noted magician, captured a piece of lightning as it struck a dead tree during a storm. He imprisoned it as a convenient way to make fire for his own use, and ignored demands that he share this wonderful discovery.

At last the tribe became so enraged with Goodah that a group of elders called up a whirlwind just as Goodah had made a fire with his piece of lightning. The whirlwind picked up the fire and scattered it all over the country, and fire became common property when members of the tribe picked up enough burning wood to make fires for themselves.

To escape the jeers and laughter of the tribe, Goodah fled to the hills to sulk, and to plan revenge.

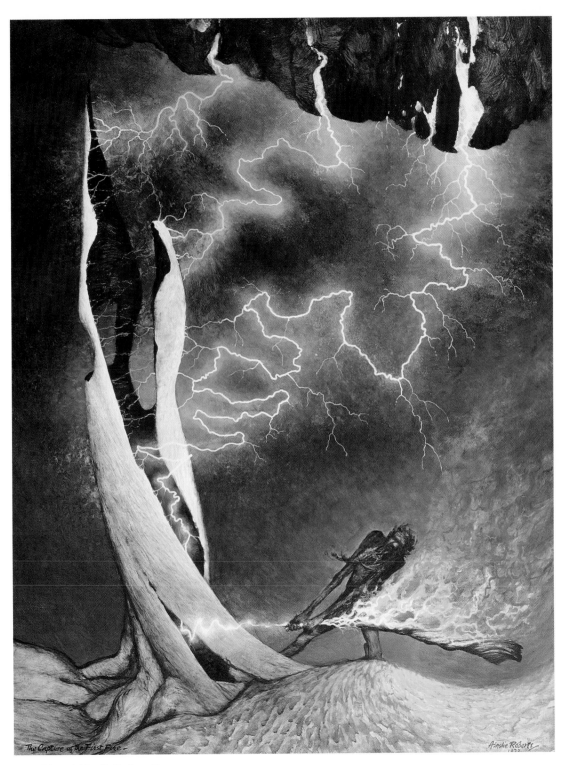

The Capture of the First Fire.

Ainslie Roberts
1973

Mr and Mrs P. C. Russell

THE SAVING OF FIRE

After Goodah lost his precious fire in the whirlwind called up by the tribal elders, the selfish magician soon thought of a way to revenge himself. He was a noted rainmaker and he began to conjure up a great storm to extinguish fire for ever.

In the tribal camp, the people were still ecstatic with excitement over the gift of fire. Without thought for the future they feasted and danced for many days, delighted with the fires that cooked their food and kept them warm.

But the wise tribal elders knew that Goodah's revenge would not be long delayed. They changed themselves into bats, and in this form they picked burning coals from the fires and flew with them to the countless trees on hills surrounding the camp. They hid coals in every tree, safe from the rain which was fire's only enemy.

They had barely completed this task before Goodah's great rainstorm came flooding over the hills. It deluged the country and put out all the tribal fires.

Cold and sorrowful, the tribesfolk gazed gloomily at the ashes until bats flittered overhead, chirping the news that the spirit of fire could now be found in every tree.

The people soon discovered this was true. When they rubbed dry wood together, the fire spirit that Goodah had made from a piece of lightning soon came to life again. And for countless centuries since then the Aborigines have made fire in that way.

The Saving of the First Fire

Miss Marcella Reale   29

THE BURNING ANT-HILL

In this myth from Melville Island two women, caught in a heavy thunderstorm, were near a tree which was shattered by a flash of lightning. After the storm, one of them picked up a piece of wood, which glowed in a manner she had never seen before. But she dropped it immediately, and called out, "Yakai! That thing bit me! It's not a snake, what can it be?"

They saw the glowing wood burst into flames, and found its heat warmed their bodies and that their meat and seed cakes tasted much better when thrown on the hot coals. The two women decided to keep their discovery to themselves. They hid the fire in a huge termite mound well away from the camp, took it out to cook their food, and hid it again afterwards.

Their two sons soon discovered this secret, and were so angry at their mothers' selfishness in not sharing this good fortune that they changed themselves into crocodiles. They waited until the women were gathering waterlily bulbs in the lagoon, then pulled them under and drowned them.

The sons, like their selfish mothers, planned to keep the fire for themselves, but when they hurried back to the great ant-hill they found that the fire was growing larger and larger. It burst from its hiding place, and the flames leapt and danced in all directions until they hid themselves in every piece of dry wood.

Since then, the Aborigines have only had to rub two dry sticks together to bring out the hidden fire, but the sons were changed back into their crocodile forms, to live in cold and gloom and never to enjoy their mothers' discovery.

THE FIRE SPREADERS

Australian Aboriginal mythology has recorded many beliefs which explain how fire was first obtained, how fire-making was perfected, and how it was used for cooking, for warmth, for lighting night ceremonies, and for many other purposes. Fire, and its benefits, was possibly the richest Dreamtime heritage of all. One of its most spectacular uses was as an aid to hunting.

At the time of the year when speargrass, spinifex, and other grasses were dry, the Aborigines set fire to them and waited for the rush of goannas, snakes, kangaroos, and wallabies escaping from the blaze. In this way they could kill game more quickly, and in larger quantities, than by any other method.

But the Aborigines were not the only ones to gain their food out of the flames. The fork-tailed kites also benefit from fires, and they have added some refinements of their own. They gather in their thousands above a grass-fire, to feed on the wing on insects rising in the thermal currents created by the heat, and to swoop on small rodents fleeing from the fire.

The Aborigines regarded these birds as masters of cunning comparable only with dingoes, for they have seen fork-tailed kites deliberately start fresh fires by picking up smouldering sticks in their claws and dropping them in distant patches of dry grass. Having used this "tool of fire," they climb and await the wild exodus of scared and half-blind insects, rodents, and reptiles that soon appears.

There is nothing in Aboriginal mythology that records whether the Aborigines or the birds first discovered how to use fire in this way, but today the fork-tailed kites still carry on a tradition that was born in the Dreamtime of the Aborigines.

Mr and Mrs B. Glowrey

KOOLULLA AND THE
TWO SISTERS

The Aborigines of southern Australia had a belief that two sisters lived deep in the ocean in a vast forest of kelp. Sometimes they came up on the shore to search for crabs and shellfish among the rocks, and on one of these occasions they were so busy at their task that they did not see that Koolulla, who was a renowned hunter, was camped near by.

Koolulla had been casting his net in the shallows, and had just finished cooking his catch when he saw the sisters. He was so impressed by their beauty that he resolved to capture them, and so he picked up his net and a large firestick from the fire and crept close enough to the two women to throw his net over them. One wriggled out from under it and jumped back into the sea. Quickly, Koolulla secured the net around his one captive and leaped into the water in chase of her sister. As his firestick sank it created a burst of sparks which floated up into the sky.

Koolulla swam all that day in pursuit of the woman, but she finally led him into the kelp forest. There, exhausted and entangled in the great mass of seaweed, he sank to the bottom and was transformed into the shark, compelled always to hunt the deep waters in search of the woman he lost.

The sister on the shore, unable to free herself from Koolulla's net, eventually died and was changed into the evening star. The sparks from Koolulla's firestick may still be seen in the sky. They are the first stars to appear as night falls, and the brightest of them all is the evening star, keeping watch over her sister who still lives in the underwater forest.

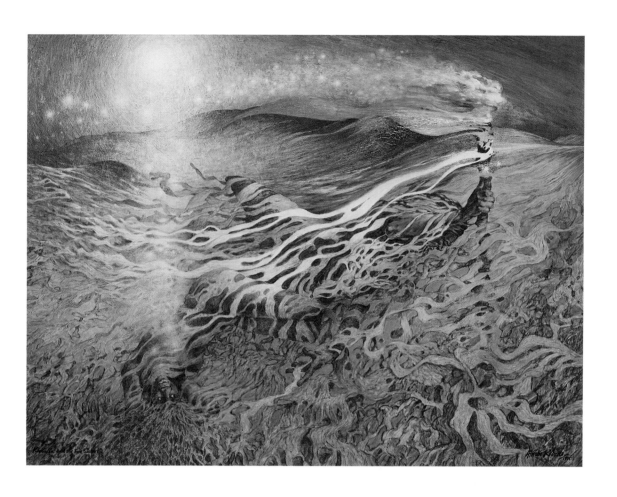

THE CREATION OF KULPUNYA

The impact of the imposing beauty and vivid colouring of Ayers Rock on a modern traveller is an unforgettable experience. The relationship between Ayers Rock and the Aborigines of the surrounding desert adds a mystical significance to this massive geological feature.

The Pitjandjara tribe believed that Ayers Rock, their Uluru, rose miraculously out of a large red sandhill. The creation of all its natural features such as the great bays, the chasms in its steep sides, the waterholes, fretted surfaces, huge pot-holes, and caves, is explained in the rich store of myths handed down from generation to generation of the Pitjandjara.

One major myth relates that, in the Dreamtime, the Mala men of Uluru and the Windulka men of Kikingura became enemies. The Windulka had invited the Mala people to attend one of their ceremonies, but received such a rude refusal that they instructed their medicine-man to create Kulpunya, a huge and evil dingo.

The medicine-man laid out a framework consisting of a mulga branch for the backbone, sticks for the ears, moles' teeth at one end and a bandicoot's tail at the other, and women's hair along the back. For many days he sang his magic songs and lethal chants over the framework, until it stirred, rose upright, and came to horrid life as Kulpunya the spirit dingo. Full of hatred and malice, Kulpunya reached Uluru so swiftly that the Mala people were taken by surprise, and most of them were killed.

Today, the camps of the Mala men and initiates are the huge fretted areas on the Rock's northern face, the Naldawatta pole used in their ceremonies is an immense semi-detached slab of rock over five hundred feet high, the initiates are the boulders at its base, and dozens of minor features of the great monolith bear witness to Kulpunya's ferocity.

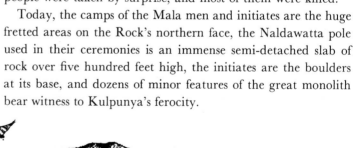

The Creation of Kalpanya

Mr and Mrs M. A. Klemich

THE CREATION OF
BLACK MOUNTAIN

The painting shown on the following two pages depicts a myth from northern Queensland. The Aborigines of the Cooktown area related how, long ago in the Dreamtime, there lived two brothers, Tajalruji and Kalruji. Since childhood they had been close companions, and in manhood they became mighty hunters. They supplied their tribe with food gained almost daily from their journeys to the tribal hunting grounds. The country in this region was flat and covered with shining black boulders.

One day, when the brothers were hunting on the farthest edge of their land, they saw a beautiful girl digging for yams. She was of the rock python totem, and would have been an acceptable mate for either of the men, who were of the wallaby totem.

In that moment, when each wanted the girl for himself, the previously inseparable brothers became enemies. They decided to fight for her, but this decision was hard to carry out. They both knew that their tribal laws forbade them to use hunting weapons against another member of the tribe. Eventually they decided that each should make a mound of the great black stones so that he who built the highest could cast a boulder down to destroy his rival.

Watched by the girl, the men toiled day after day until two huge piles rose from the plain. First one and then the other would be just a little taller, but not enough for either brother to cast the final boulder. So preoccupied were they with the deadly task that neither of them saw the first shreds of cloud that Kakahinka, the cyclone, flew as a warning that he was near.

The cyclone struck, and in its devastation the two brothers died on their mounds of stones. The girl was blown away by the wind and lost in the tangle of boulders and vegetation left in the wake of the cyclone.

Today, the great mass of stones still remains and is known as Black Mountain, or the Mountain of Death. The story explains why the only living creatures to be found there are the huge rock pythons and the black wallabies.

Hans Looser of Cooktown, who recorded this myth, describes Black Mountain as "the most evil place in Australia". The mountain of black boulders, two miles long and 1,000 feet high, rises bare and sinister out of the tropical rainforests a few miles south of the old gold-mining port. Honeycombed with caves and tunnels, it has always been a place of tragedy. A man was first recorded as having disappeared there in 1877, and since then eleven men are known to have ventured on to Black Mountain and vanished without trace. Straying cattle and horses have also disappeared. No vegetation grows on the slopes of the mountain, birds and animals shun the area, and the Aborigines would never approach it.

Mrs Dale Roberts

41

THE MIMICS

In the great creation period of the Australian Aborigines, the animals and the birds enjoyed a common language. In their communal life there were no sorrows and no antagonism, and always there was an abundance of food. Each year they held many corroborees and feasts.

But at one of these gatherings the frog, who in those days was a wonderful mimic, started imitating the voices of his companions. He was so pleased with his efforts, and at the perfection of his gift, that he could not stop. He went on and on, making ruder and ruder remarks until many quarrels and fights broke out.

The eagle, the native cat, the kangaroo, the platypus, the goanna, and the crow all seemed to be hurling insults at each other, until the frog, in the voice of the wombat, called out "To battle, to battle," and in the resultant fight many creatures were killed or hurt. Only the lyrebird took no part in the uproar, and tried in vain to stop it.

This fighting annoyed the spirits so much that they took away the common language and made each creature adopt a language of its own. But as a reward for the lyrebird's part in the affair, the spirits gave it the power to imitate all the animals, birds, reptiles, and insects.

And so the lyrebird became the greatest mimic of all, and the Aborigines took care not to annoy it. They knew, through their mythology, that what had happened because of the frog might well happen again if the lyrebird was not kept in a happy frame of mind.

The Mimics.

Sir Robert Helpmann

JARAPA AND THE
MAN OF WOOD

Jarapa, a man of the Waddaman tribe in the long-distant past, fancied himself as a magician and tried to create a human being. He cut a piece of wood from a tree, shaped it to look like the body of a man, and added sticks for the arms and legs, and rounded stones for the knee and arm joints. All day and night Jarapa beat his tap sticks and sang a secret song over the image until his voice became hoarse, but it did not respond. At last Jarapa gave up in disgust and walked away.

But he had not gone far when he heard the crashing of trees behind him, and he saw that the man of wood, grown hugely, had come to life and was following him. A white cockatoo clung to the monster and screeched warnings to all creatures in its path.

Terrified, Jarapa could not escape the man of wood until he realised that it was pursuing him by sight only. It became confused when Jarapa was out of sight. So he hid behind a large rock, and his creation blundered past and at last disappeared over the horizon.

For countless generations of Aborigines, the spirit of Jarapa's man of wood was known as the Wulgaru, the self-appointed judge of the dead. Some believe that it still wanders around northern Australia in search of its creator.

Jaraca and the Man of Word

BIRTH OF THE MOOGOORA

In the Dreamtime of the Encounter Bay tribe of South Australia, an old man called Lime was visited by a friend, Palpangye, who brought him some bream, a river fish not then known in the area. Lime returned the favour by giving Palpangye some sea mullet he had caught that day. As the men sat by the camp-fire after eating the two kinds of fish, Lime told his friend he had enjoyed the bream so much that he wished there were rivers in the neighborhood, so that he might catch bream for himself.

So that night Palpangye, who was a noted man of magic, went into the hills and pulled a huge dead gum tree out of the ground. He turned it upside down, then thrust it into the earth and twisted it round and round. Water and fish flowed up and filled the hole he had made.

Palpangye did this in many places, and the great pools over-flowed into each other until the water formed the Moogoora river and reached the sea. He then walked some distance to the east, where he created the Yalladoola river in the same way. These are the rivers known today as the Inman and the Hind-marsh, and they are still favourite breeding waters for bream.

When the time came for the old men to die, Palpangye transformed himself into a bird. Lime became a large rock on the shores of the bay, and the sea in its vicinity has ever since abounded in mullet. The myth records that women and children were never allowed to tread on the rock, but old people, because of their long acquaintance with Lime, were allowed to do so.

Birth of the Mongoose.   Ainslie Roberts

Private Collection

THE OLD MAN AND
HIS SIX SONS

Tonanga, the narrator of this myth, was Albert Namatjira, who related that the Aranda tribe originated in the Creation days when an old man started out on a long journey from a cave in Haasts Bluff. He carried a big churinga stone, a spear, and a spear-thrower. Six namatoona (smaller copies of the churinga) were his sons, which he carried in a dilly-bag round his neck.

When the old man wanted his sons to hunt for meat he took the namatoona out of the dilly-bag and rubbed them with goanna fat. This magic caused them to stand up as six men, each with a spear and spear-thrower.

For a long, long time the old man wandered over a large part of Central Australia. Each time he met a group of women, the old man instructed them to prepare six camps for he had six sons to give to them in marriage. When the old man decided it was time to move on, he changed his sons back into namatoona stones and put them in his dilly-bag.

Always that old man travelled on, carrying his churinga, his spear and spear-thrower, and his six namatoona. Always he gave his six sons in marriage to the women he met. But at last he became very old and very tired, and died.

He made his last camp and lay down with his dilly-bag beside him. When the old man was dead, the six namatoona wanted to get out. They started to roll about in the dilly-bag, and the dilly-bag rolled round and round in a circle. The old man turned into a stone, and underneath that stone is a big churinga. And close to it is a smaller stone which is the dilly-bag with the six namatoona inside.

The Fertility Stones

Dr and Mrs M. E. Nancarrow

49

THE TRANSFORMATION
OF BURNBA

The hawk-man, Wabula, was without a wife. One day he visited a neighboring tribe and was attracted to an unmarried girl, Burnba. Wabula went to the near-by beach, caught some lobsters, and cooked them. Then he returned to the camp and offered them to the girl who, much to his disgust, would have nothing to do with him.

Wabula was determined to capture her. He retired to a spot out of sight and hearing of the camp, and there he built a bark hut. That night he returned to the sleeping camp and carried Burnba away by force, placed her in the hut, and blocked up all the openings so that she could not escape.

Afraid and lonely, Burnba cried all night for her father to help her. He was a skilled magician and had a spear-thrower with which he had performed many wonders. The first time he rubbed it, a heavy wind sprang up and grew stronger and stronger. It blew violently upon the bark hut, which shook so much that cracks appeared in it everywhere. The magician rubbed the spear-thrower a second time, and transformed his daughter into a butterfly. In this form she was able to escape through one of the cracks.

At last the wind lifted the bark hut off the ground and Wabula discovered that Burnba had gone. Still yearning for the girl, he changed himself into a hawk, so that he and Burnba could always live in the same element.

"The Transformation of Buraba"

Ainslie Roberts
1972

BARACUMA'S FISHING NET

In a myth from South Australia, Baracuma owned the only fishing net in the world. It was so good that when he cast it into the water the net immediately filled with fish. Wandi, a friend from a neighbouring tribe, heard the story of the wonderful net and begged Baracuma to allow him to use it.

Baracuma refused to lend the net, because he knew that if it was out of his possession for any length of time he would die. Wandi pleaded with Baracuma, assuring him that he would return the net promptly. Baracuma, persuaded against his better judgement, allowed Wandi to take the net away.

However, the fish were so plentiful that Wandi forgot his promise until darkness forced him to return the net. To his dismay, he found that Baracuma was dead. He tried all night to bring his friend back to life, but without success.

Wandi was so ashamed over the result of his selfishness that he changed himself into a hawk and flew to the top of a high tree.

An old Kangaroo-man heard that Baracuma had died for his generosity, and used magical powers to restore him to life in the form of a native cat.

The Aborigines believed that this is why Wandi the hawk lives and nests high in the treetops, and hunts for his food during the day, while Baracuma the native cat avoids the selfish Wandi by making his home underground and catching lizards and other small creatures during the hours of darkness.

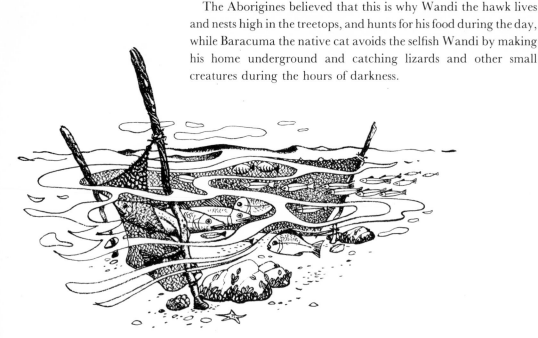

Baradenna's Fishing Net

Ainslie Roberts
1972

THE SONGMAN AND THE
TWO SUNS

During the long-distant past, Junkgao, a mythical creator, his wife Walo the sun-woman, her daughter Bara, and his sister Madalait, lived in a country to the east of Arnhem Land.

One day, Junkgao and his sister Madalait set out in their bark canoe to cross the sea to Arnhem Land. As they neared their destination, they enjoyed the lines of light that were reflected from the crests of the waves and the beauty of the long white sandhills on the distant shore. They thought these sandhills resembled the waves of the sea.

At the same time, Walo the sun-woman and her daughter Bara rose in the east to make their daily journey across the sky. But Walo always sent her daughter back, being afraid that the heat of two suns in the sky at one time would not only scorch the hair of the Aborigines, but might even set the whole world on fire.

The early morning spectacle so pleased Junkgao that he composed many songs on the beauties about him; the sunrise, the light on the crests of the waves, the sound of the waves breaking on the beach, and the parallel lines of white sandhills.

At the same time, Junkgao decreed that the lines of light on the waves, and the lines of the sandhills, should be his sacred marks and those of his descendants for ever.

Songman and the Two Suns

BIRTH OF THE BUTTERFLIES

When the world was young, the birds and animals had a common language and there was no death. No creature had any experience of its mystery, until one day a young cockatoo fell from a tree and broke its neck. The birds and animals could not wake it, and a meeting of the wise ones decided that the spirits had taken back the bird to change it into another form.

Everyone thought this a reasonable explanation, but to prove the theory the leaders called for volunteers who would imitate the dead cockatoo by going up into the sky for a whole winter. During this time, they would not be allowed to see, hear, smell, or taste anything. In the spring they were to return to earth to relate their experiences to the others. The caterpillars offered to try this experiment, and went up in the sky into a huge cloud.

On the first warm day of spring a pair of excited dragonflies told the gathering that the caterpillars were returning with new bodies. Soon the dragonflies led back into the camp a great pageant of white, yellow, red, blue, and green creatures—the first butterflies, and proof that the spirits had changed the caterpillars' bodies into another form.

They clustered in large groups on the trees and bushes, and everything looked so gay and colourful that the wise ones decided this was a good and happy thing that had happened, and decreed it must always be so. Since then caterpillars always spend winter hidden in cocoons, preparing for their dramatic change into one of spring's most beautiful symbols.

CONDULA AND BAK-BAK

Long years ago, an old Aboriginal made a cloak from the skin of a red kangaroo for his young daughter Condula. This gift made Condula very happy, for it was more beautiful than any of the cloaks owned by other tribeswomen. As she took the gift, she was told that as soon as her lover Bak-bak had completed his training for tribal manhood, they could be married.

Every evening, when Condula finished her food-gathering, she climbed to the top of an isolated rock to watch for the return of her lover; and every evening the heart of Bak-bak was gladdened by the sight of that red-cloaked figure waiting for his return.

But one night Condula was sad, for she heard that Bak-bak, together with other young men of the tribe, had been sent out to fight some enemies who were trespassing on their land. Again she climbed the pillar of stone, this time to watch for the return of the warriors, but Bak-bak was not among them. Visualising her lover lying silent and still on an open plain, she refused to leave her lonely post. Finally, in her grief, she died.

The body of Bak-bak was changed into the rock on which Condula had spent so many happy hours watching for her lover to come back from the hunt, and so many hopeless hours waiting for his return from the battle.

Condula and her red cloak were transformed into a beautiful waratah that grew up beside the rock so that, even in death, the lovers were not separated.

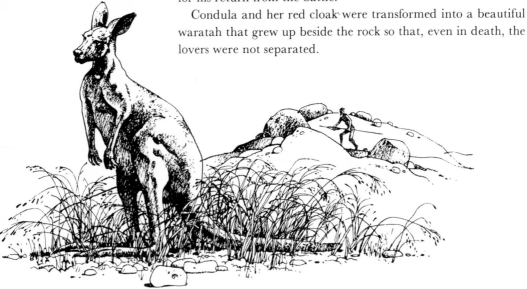

THUNDERSTORMS

The Aborigines of northern Australia have a number of myths that explain the thunder, the lightning, the wet-season clouds, and the rain.

On Melville Island it is a woman, Bumerali, who strikes the ground with her stone axes mounted on long flexible handles. These are the lightning flashes which destroy the trees and sometimes the Aborigines.

The Arnhem Land Aborigines believe that the thunder-man, Jambuwul, travels from place to place on the large cumulus clouds of the wet season, shedding the life-giving rain on the earth beneath. These thunder-clouds are also the home of tiny spirit children, the yurtus, who travel on the raindrops to descend to earth and find a human mother.

The painting is an interpretation of a myth from further south, where the Aborigines describe how their thunder-man, Mamaragan, lives in the wet-season clouds, and how the billows of clouds that form on the summits of those clouds are huge white boulders.

In the wet season Mamaragan, with roars of laughter, beats the great stones of the sky together. His laughter is the rolling thunder; the sharper crack of lightning is the sound of the stones striking each other; the lightning is the sparks flying from them. The rain caused by this disturbance falls to the thirsty earth and gives life and food to mankind and all other creatures.

The Thunder Stones.

THE VOICE OF NATURE

The Australian Aborigines' complete identification with their environment was not only their solution to the problem of survival but also a rich and rewarding spiritual experience. The great Ancestral Being of the creation period—the Dreamtime—made their world and all forms of life, and dictated the laws and patterns of behaviour that governed their tribal life. They felt secure in a belief that the voice of their creative Ancestor spoke to them in everything.

But they were not always faithful to this belief. An Aboriginal myth from southern Australia relates how, in the beginning, the voice of the Ancestor spoke each day from a great gum tree, and the tribe gathered around to listen. But as time went by the people grew weary of hearing his words of wisdom. One by one they turned their backs on the voice to pursue their own pleasures, and a vast silence settled over the whole of the land and the sea. There was no wind and the tides were still, no birds sang, and the earth seemed to be dying.

The tribe soon wearied of the pleasures of their own making and began to be afraid and lonely. They returned to the great tree again and again, hoping to hear the words that would ease their misery. And one day the voice of their Ancestor spoke again.

He told them it was the last time his voice would be heard, but that he would give them a sign. The great tree split open, a huge tongue of light came down into its trunk, and then it closed up again.

Since that time the Aborigines have known that the voice of their Ancestor exists in all things, and speaks to them through every part of nature.

The Widow Maker, Granite Stone

Ainslie Roberts

Mr and Mrs R. W. Griffiths

IN THE BEGINNING

The storytellers, who handed down the beliefs from generation to generation, preserved the wealth of detail about the Aborigines' concepts of the creation of life. All their creation myths were based on an Ancestral Being, but the details and name of this creator varied between different tribes.

In the desert areas in the west of South Australia, the Aborigines explain how their creator, Bunjil, made the world and all things on it. First he made the sun, the moon, and the stars. Then he made the hills, the valleys, the great plains, and all the trees and plants. Next he created all the creatures to inhabit the land.

Having done all this, Bunjil became lonely. He felt the need for companions with whom to sing and dance, and so he decided to make a man. He searched for the finest clay, fashioned a man to his own likeness, and added some finely-shredded tree-bark for the hair. Bunjil was so pleased with his creation that he immediately made another.

When both figures were finished he breathed on them to give them life. His breath was a wind of great violence that blew for many days and swept every growing thing from that area. When the land grew still again the two figures came to life, and the clay that was left over became the oddly-shaped rocks that are in the region today.

Bunjil stayed with the two men for a long time. He taught them to sing and dance, and under his guidance they gradually became wise in all things. Eventually they, in their turn, could pass on Bunjil's wisdom to all the Aborigines who followed them.

CREATION OF THE
COORONG BIRDS

During the Dreamtime, when all the birds were still Aborigines, they had a favourite fishing spot near the Murray mouth. When they used their nets they worked as a team, and the only man who was a misfit was the Magpie-man. He was lazy and disliked the water. It was his duty to carry the firesticks so that a fire could be made to cook the fish.

One cold day, after the men in the water had made a good catch, they called out to the Magpie-man to build a fire, so that they could warm themselves and cook the fish. But the lazy Magpie-man, being away from the water and not feeling cold, said there was not enough wood about to build a fire and urged the others to go on fishing.

This happened again and again, until the disgusted fishermen waded ashore and made their own fire. When all the cod, mulloway, and perch had been shared, the only fish left were bony bream. These are so bony that they were seldom eaten, and so the fishermen gave them to the Magpie-man as punishment for his laziness.

This so angered the Magpie-man that he took a bream in each hand and attacked the rest of the party. In the commotion that followed the men turned themselves into birds, and many of them were splashed white with flying scales.

The pelican, his previously black body now partly white, jumped into the water, and the net he once carried was changed into the large pouch under his bill. The cormorants and ducks dived under water to escape harm, and the coots ran into the reeds. The magpie, his black body also marked with the silvery scales, flew to the top of a cliff. To this day he keeps away from the water and the fishing birds with whom he once quarrelled.

Creation of the Wading Birds

Ainslie Roberts 1972

THE ISLAND OF SPEARS

The Murrumbidgee River was once the dividing boundary between two tribes. Each group respected the laws of the other, but there came a day when Gobba-gumbalin, a young warrior from the southern tribe, spoke to Pomin-galana, a young woman of the neighbouring tribe who was swimming by the bank.

After this they took every opportunity to meet, even though the woman was promised to a warrior of her own tribe. Their desire for each other became so strong that they planned to run away to the near-by hills, where they hoped they would be safe from the vengeance of both tribes.

Their love was so strong that they became incautious, and both tribes came to know of their nightly meetings. The elders decided that, for the sake of tribal peace, the lovers should be destroyed. So on the night when they swam to meet each other in the centre of the river, intending to escape by swimming downstream, many spearmen from both tribes were hidden in the reeds lining each bank. Just as the lovers reached each other they were pierced by a hail of spears and sank to the river bottom.

Today, a reed-covered island in mid-river marks the spot where they died. The Aborigines say that the reeds are the spears that killed the lovers; that the red cliffs further downstream were stained by their blood; and that the frogs on either side of the river still mourn their fate, because those on one side call "Gobba-gumbalin," and the frogs on the opposite bank reply with the sound of "Pomin-galana."

'The Island of Spears' Amelie Roberts
1974

Commander and Mrs R. Brasch

THE FIRST DAWN

The Aborigines of the Dieyerie tribe, in the far north of South Australia, believed that all living creatures were created by Pirra, the moon. This task was carried out under the direction of the Mooramoora, the great spirit who made all things. Pirra created man by first making two small black lizards. He then divided their feet into toes and fingers and, with a forefinger, formed the noses, eyes, ears, and mouths. Pirra placed the creatures in a standing position, which they could not retain, and so he cut off their tails and the lizards walked erect. They were then made male and female, to perpetuate the race.

But when these first men and women began to move about the land, guided only by the moon's light, they found it dark and bitterly cold because the sun had not been created. Hunting weapons had not been developed, and the small animals they caught for food had to be run down on foot.

The biggest creature in that far-off Dreamtime was the emu. It was many times larger than it is now, and the hunters knew that the flesh of an emu, could they but capture one, would provide food for the tribe for a long time. They made many attempts to capture the big bird, but it was so fast, and the world so dark and cold, that they never succeeded. The emu always vanished into the darkness.

So the hunters held a great gathering, performed many ceremonies, and pleaded with Mooramoora to make their world warmer and lighter so that they could capture the emu. And Mooramoora listened to their troubles and made the sun, thus creating day and night.

The First Dawn —

Ainslie Roberts 1975

THE WEEPING OPAL

A myth of central Queensland relates that in the days of the Dreamtime, when the world was young and the great creation events were taking place, a giant opal ruled over the destinies of men and women. This Ancestral Being lived in the sky, made the laws under which the tribes should live, and dictated the punishments to be inflicted on those who broke the laws.

The creation of this Aboriginal Ancestor came about as a result of a war between two tribes. The fighting had gone on for so long that, at last, the combatants had broken or lost all their weapons. So they began hurling boulders at each other, and a tribesman threw one so hard that it flew upwards and lodged in the sky.

The boulder grew rapidly as the frightened warriors watched, until it burst open and revealed the flashing colours of a huge opal. And as the opal saw the dead and wounded warriors lying on the ground below, it wept in sorrow.

Tears streamed from the opal in such profusion that they became a great rainstorm, and when the sun shone on the opal-coloured tears the Aborigines saw their first rainbow.

From that time on, the Aborigines of that area believed the rainbow was a sign that someone had committed a crime against the tribal laws laid down so long ago, and that the tears of the opal were again falling in sorrow.

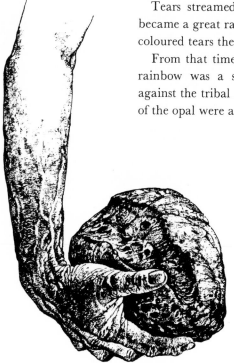

NARUWILYA AND THE INTRUDER

In the early days of the world a human creator, Naruwilya, made his home in the rugged and inhospitable Wessell Islands of north-western Arnhem Land.

After a while Naruwilya became dissatisfied with human existence. He was attracted by the colour and life of the sea, and so he changed himself into a fish. But even this did not suit him, so he took the form of an octopus and spent his time searching for food among the outcrops of coral.

Finally he decided that the trees and the open sky would make the best home of all, and so he transformed himself into a flying fox. He has remained in that form ever since.

On the Wessell Islands there is a place where flying foxes live. This area is forbidden to all Aborigines. Should anyone trespass there, and particularly if he should injure or kill one of the flying foxes, Naruwilya will change himself again into an octopus, enter the body of the intruder, wrap his tentacles around his heart, and kill him.

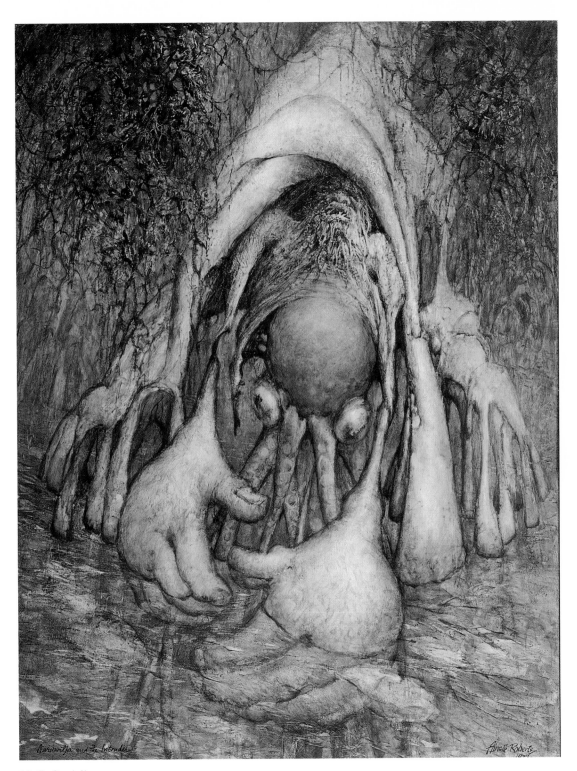

Mr B. Consiglio

THE RAINBOW SERPENT

In the mythology of the Australian Aborigines, the most widespread of their beliefs was in the existence of a huge serpent which lived in waterholes, swamps, and lakes. In most myths it was associated with the rainbow. Rainbow-serpent myths were Australia-wide, but the greatest variety came from northern Australia, where the thunder-clouds and violent rains of the monsoonal season provided the ideal environment.

The Rainbow-serpent myths vary widely in their telling, and in the names given to the serpent, but the creatures themselves had many characteristics in common.

Most myths describe a huge snake that spent the dry season resting in a deep waterhole. In the wet season, it went up into the sky as a rainbow. It was of immense size, brilliant in colouring, and often had a mane and a beard. Usually it was an object of fear to the Aborigines, especially when resting in its waterhole, and the greatest care was taken not to annoy or offend the mighty snake. Should anyone disturb its rest, the Rainbow-serpent would inevitably create some disaster, from simply eating the offender to making the waterhole overflow and thus drowning everyone in the world.

In some myths, Rainbow-serpents appear as Ancestral Creators. Their bodies contained not only the first Aborigines, but all the natural features of the land which in that remote time was flat and featureless. In others, the appearance of a rainbow meant that the serpent was travelling from one waterhole to another. Sometimes it was linked with the rainbow colours of quartz crystals, which the medicine-men of many tribes used as objects of magic.

But whatever its shape or name or habits, the Rainbow-serpent was an awesome creature of power and importance.

77

THE STORYTELLER

Since the dawn of time, Aboriginal elders have been the storytellers who have handed down the Dreamtime myths. The creation myths say that, in the beginning, no life existed in the world. It was void: without form and in darkness.

Then the Great Creators appeared. Each creation myth describes the journey of a Creator through the Dreamtime world. As he travelled, he gave topographic features to the world, created natural forces, and created life in all its forms, including the Aboriginal people. A number of myths relate the way in which a Creator made mankind in his own image.

The Creators also established the tribal laws which govern the conduct of Aboriginal society, so that its members would live in harmony. They decreed that everyone should partake of food caught by the hunters, and that a hunter should always take a lesser share. His reward was to be the satisfaction of achievement. The laws also stressed the importance of the family group and gave all members of the tribe an equal responsibility for the care of the aged.

When the Dreamtime creation figures had completed their work on earth, many of them made their homes in the sky and became the sun, moon, and stars.

The Dreamtime mythology does not attribute all power to a single God, nor does it tell of a Son who came in human form, but throughout the pattern of the myths passed on by Aboriginal storytellers are woven many threads which resemble the Christian commandments and beliefs in creation.

If we are prepared to study these myths with an open mind, we will find that the apparent gulf between the two cultures is not as wide and impassable as it may seem.

ACKNOWLEDGMENTS

Many of the myths in this volume are printed for the first time. Others have appeared in numerous versions over the past 125 years and every effort has been made to discover their origins. The fact that different tribes used variations of some basic myths, and that early European writers interpreted these in many different styles and ways, has made it difficult to ascertain the dates and authors of the first versions to be published in English. The sources listed are the earliest that can be traced, and grateful acknowledgment is given to those who have granted permission to use such sources as reference. In some cases it has not been possible to trace either the author or the publisher of the original material.

The debt to the Australian Aborigines, who originated and perpetuated these myths of their Dreamtime, is most gratefully acknowledged.

SOURCES

Australian Inland Mission Frontier Services. *The Storyteller*. Unpublished ms., 1975.

HARNEY, W. E. *Tales from the Aborigines*. Robert Hale, London, 1959.

LOCKWOOD, DOUGLAS. *Northern Territory Sketchbook*. Rigby, Adelaide, 1968.

LOOSER, HANS. *The Mountains of Death*. Privately printed, Cooktown, n.d.

McKEOWN, KEITH C. *Land of the Byamee*. Randle House, Sydney, 1938.

MATHEWS, R. H. *Mythology of the Gundungurra Tribe*. Folk-Lore Society, London, 1909.

MOUNTFORD, CHARLES P. *Arnhem Land; Art, Myth and Symbolism*. Melbourne University Press, Melbourne, 1956.

——. *Ayers Rock; Its People, Their Beliefs, Their Art*. Angus & Robertson, Sydney, 1965.

——. *The Fishermen of the Lakes*. Unpublished ms., 1960.

——. *The Native Cat and the Hawk*. Unpublished ms., 1960.

——. *The Discovery of Fire*. Unpublished ms., 1960.

PECK, C. W. *Australian Legends*. Stafford & Co., Sydney, 1925.

ROBINSON, ROLAND. *Aboriginal Myths and Legends*. Sun Books, Sydney, 1966.

SMITH, W. RAMSAY. *Myths and Legends of the Australian Aboriginals*. George G. Harrap, London, 1930.

TURNER, R. *Australian Jungle Stories*. Northwood Press, Camperdown, Victoria, 1936.

WOODS, J. D. (ed.). *The Native Tribes of South Australia*. E. S. Wigg & Son, Adelaide, 1879.